CONTENTS

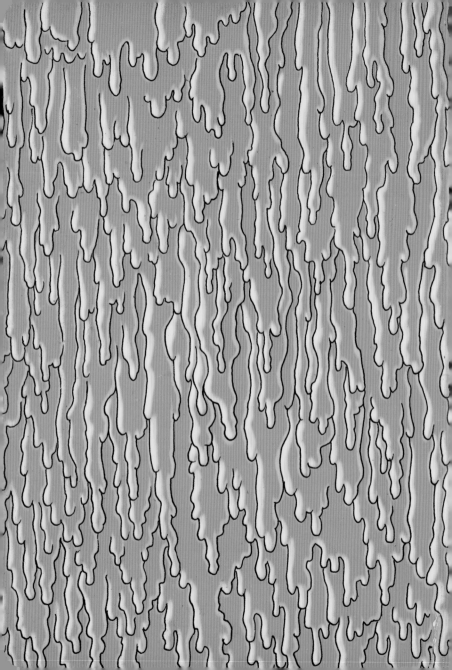

WHAT A BLAST!

VILE VOLCANOES

ANITA GANERI

MIKE PHILLIPS

013401993X

"This is a horribly good way to show that
learning about our world can be fun.
And seriously important."

Michael Palin

Scholastic Children's Books,
Euston House, 24 Eversholt Street,
London, NW1 1DB, UK

A division of Scholastic Ltd
London ~ New York ~ Toronto ~ Sydney ~ Auckland
Mexico City ~ New Delhi ~ Hong Kong

Editorial Director: Lisa Edwards
Senior Editor: Jill Sawyer

First published in the UK by Scholastic Ltd, 2010

ISBN 978 1407105 84 0

Printed and bound by Tien Wah Press Pte. Ltd, Malaysia

2 4 6 8 10 9 7 5 3 1

INTRODUCTION

Is your life dull as ditchwater? Is tormenting your little sister boring you to tears? Fancy the adventure of a lifetime? Well, you've come to the right place. You're about to embark on an earth-shattering expedition to some of the hottest spots on Planet Earth. Yep, we're talking vile volcanoes, and they don't come much hotter than that. But if the wildest place you've ever been is your back garden on a windy day, DON'T PANIC. This horribly useful handbook is your sure-fire guide to some of the world's vilest volcanoes and how to survive if they suddenly blow their tops. Think you can stand the heat?

So, read on to find out…
• how to spot an active volcano (without getting blown up)
• what *not* to do if you smell rotten eggs
• how to stop a lethal lava flow
• when to call upon a volcano saint
• which volcano you can take a dip in

And that's not all. This handy book's packed with hair-raising true stories about people who found themselves in horribly hot water when a volcano blew. Not to mention life-saving survival tips from real-life vulcanologists (they're scientists who study volcanoes) trying to get to grips with what makes volcanoes tick.

But be warned. You'll need to be brave. Visiting vile volcanoes is no picnic. For a start, they're horribly unpredictable. A volcano that's simmered away happily for centuries can suddenly go off with a bang. And despite having loads of new-fangled kit, vulcanologists can't always say for certain when a volcano's going to erupt next. Worse still, even if they predict an eruption, there's nothing on Earth they can do to stop it. So you'll need to keep your wits about you and your eyes peeled for warning signs. Then you can get outta there … fast. Still keen to pay a volcano a visit? Oh well, at least you'll be going out with a bang.

VILE VOLCANOES

It's one of the most dramatic events in nature (as long as you don't get too close). A vile volcano that's begun to erupt. Ask someone to describe a volcano and they'll most likely mutter something about a cone-shaped mountain that spurts out red-hot rock. But volcanoes don't all look like that. Some volcanoes are simply cracks in the ground where lava oozes out. Some puff away quietly for centuries. Others suddenly explode with a colossal bang. So what on Earth is a vile volcano, and what on Earth makes it lose its cool? Keep reading to find out the answers to these burning questions. This chapter's packed with useful information about vile volcanoes and their horrible habits.

VILE VOLCANO FACT FILE

Name: VOLCANO

What it is: CRACK IN THE GROUND FROM WHICH RED-HOT LIQUID ROCK (MAGMA) SPURTS OUT. (WHEN MAGMA REACHES THE SURFACE, IT'S CALLED LAVA. GOT THAT?)

WHERE IT HAPPENS:

a) The EARTH'S made of layers. Here's the inside story...

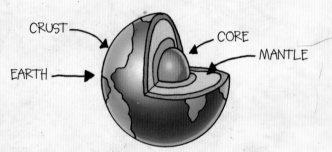

CORE: Solid ball of iron and nickel, surrounded by boiling liquid metal.

Temperature: 4,500°C. Thickness: 3,550 km.

MANTLE: Thick layer of rock that's partially melted into magma.

Temperature: 1,980°C. Thickness: 2,900 km.

CRUST: Solid layer of rock that's cracked into chunks, called plates.

Thickness: 50-70 km (on land); 5 km (on seabed).

b) The chunks of crust (plates) float on the red-hot rock underneath.

c) Sometimes, the plates are pulled further and further apart, and magma rises up to plug the gap. Loads of volcanoes happen like this but they mostly simmer away under the sea.

d) Sometimes, plates collide and one plate's dragged under another. It melts and makes magma that rises up and erupts. And here's how it happens:

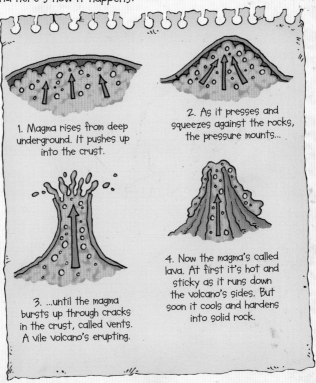

1. Magma rises from deep underground. It pushes up into the crust.

2. As it presses and squeezes against the rocks, the pressure mounts...

3. ...until the magma bursts up through cracks in the crust, called vents. A vile volcano's erupting.

4. Now the magma's called lava. At first it's hot and sticky as it runs down the volcano's sides. But soon it cools and hardens into solid rock.

Note: A third type of volcano's called a hot spot volcano and it's got nothing to do with pootling plates. Check out page 50 for some hot-spot highlights.

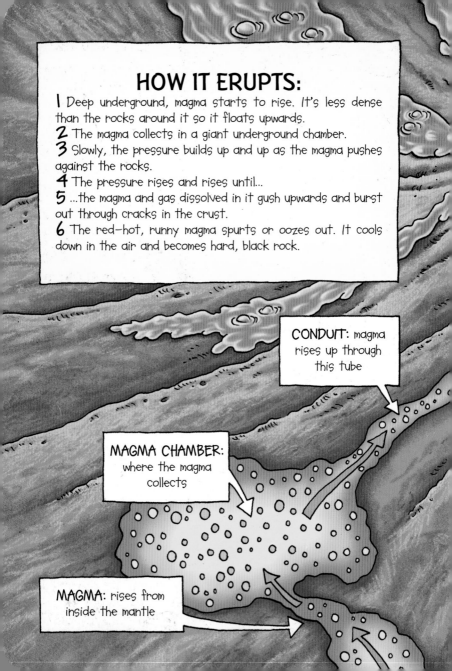

HOW IT ERUPTS:

1 Deep underground, magma starts to rise. It's less dense than the rocks around it so it floats upwards.

2 The magma collects in a giant underground chamber.

3 Slowly, the pressure builds up and up as the magma pushes against the rocks.

4 The pressure rises and rises until...

5 ...the magma and gas dissolved in it gush upwards and burst out through cracks in the crust.

6 The red-hot, runny magma spurts or oozes out. It cools down in the air and becomes hard, black rock.

CONDUIT: magma rises up through this tube

MAGMA CHAMBER: where the magma collects

MAGMA: rises from inside the mantle

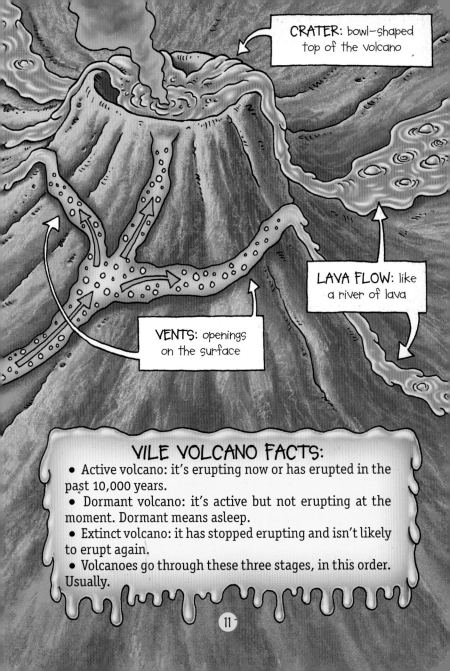

CRATER: bowl-shaped top of the volcano

LAVA FLOW: like a river of lava

VENTS: openings on the surface

VILE VOLCANO FACTS:

- Active volcano: it's erupting now or has erupted in the past 10,000 years.
- Dormant volcano: it's active but not erupting at the moment. Dormant means asleep.
- Extinct volcano: it has stopped erupting and isn't likely to erupt again.
- Volcanoes go through these three stages, in this order. Usually.

EARTH–SHATTERING FACT

Legend says volcanoes got their vile-sounding name from Vulcan, the Roman god of fire. He lived on the island of Vulcano in Italy, deep inside a flaming mountain. Smouldering sparks and rumbling noises came from this freaky peak. These were believed to be Vulcan hard at work on his forge, turning out weapons for the other gods.

Rogues gallery: volcanoes

NAME: **SHIELD VOLCANO**

Distinguishing features: Wide and low; gently sloping sides.
Explosive examples: Kilauea/Mauna Loa, Hawaii; Skjaldbreid, Iceland.

FIERY FACTS:

• They're made of layers of thin, runny lava that flows up to 100 km before cooling and going hard.
• They're named after the shape of the shields carried by ancient Icelandic warriors.
• They're sometimes topped by colossal craters that fill with lava to make lava lakes.

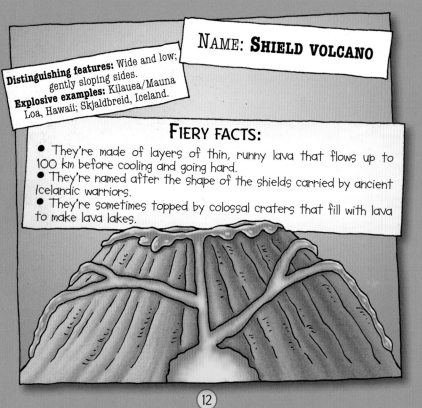

NAME: **LAVA DOME**

Distinguishing features: Stubby, dome-like shape; steep sides.
Explosive examples: Lassen's Peak, USA; Mount Merapi, Java; Soufriere Hills, Montserrat.

FIERY FACTS:

● They're made from thick, pasty lava that's slowly squeezed out like toothpaste and is too sticky to flow very far.
● They sometimes grow in the craters of other volcanoes after a major eruption (like the one at Mount St Helens).
● They sometimes collapse into a lethal heap of red-hot rock, gas and ash.

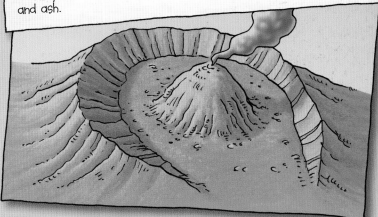

SURVIVAL TIP

If you're planning to visit a lava dome, wait for a dry day. Vulcanologists reckon heavy rain can trigger an eruption. How? Well, the rain can cause the dome to collapse, sending a massive cloud of rubble crashing down the mountainsides.

NAME: **CINDER CONE**

Distinguishing features:
Small, cone-shaped; very steep sides.
Explosive examples: Paricutin, Mexico; Sunset Crater, USA; Cerro Negro, Nicaragua.

FIERY FACTS:

- They're made from blobs of lava blown violently into the air. The blobs break up and fall as cinders around the volcano's vent.
- They can crop up in clusters of 100 cones or more.
- They're often found perching on the sides of other volcanoes, like stratovolcanoes.

Distinguishing features: Tall, symmetrical cone; steep sides.
Explosive examples: Mount Fuji, Japan; Mount Vesuvius, Italy; Mount Mayon, Philippines.

FIERY FACTS:

• They're built of layers of loose lava and ash from explosive eruptions that happened over thousands of years.
• They can be more than 3 km tall and have glaciers growing on their parky peaks.
• They're horribly explosive but luckily they don't blow their tops very often.

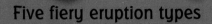

Five fiery eruption types

1 HAWAIIAN

NAMED AFTER: Hawaii (Pacific Ocean islands)
DEADLY DETAILS:
• Gentle eruption, oozing out thin, runny lava that often flows for tens of kilometres before it cools down.
• Sometimes lava gushes out in fabulous red-hot fountains that can reach over a kilometre in height.
• This type of eruption builds up whopping shield volcanoes, like those on Hawaii and Iceland.
DANGER RATING: Low

2 STROMBOLIAN

NAMED AFTER: Stromboli, Italy
DEADLY DETAILS:
• Small, explosive eruptions that go up with a loud bang, shooting chunks of lava tens or even hundreds of metres into the air.
• In between eruptions, the volcano rests for anything from a minute to half an hour or more.
• Stromboli itself is an active volcano that's erupted off and on for around 100 years.
DANGER RATING: Low/Medium

3 VULCANIAN

NAMED AFTER: Vulcano, Italy

DEADLY DETAILS:
• Highly explosive because the magma's very sticky and full of gas so the pressure builds up and explodes.
• They belch out sooty columns of black ash that can reach heights of 20 km above the ground.
• They also chuck up bread-crust bombs, but they're not tasty to eat. They're round blobs of lava that are hot and gooey inside with a hard crust, like a loaf.

DANGER RATING: High

4 PELEEAN

NAMED AFTER: Mont Pelee, Martinique

DEADLY DETAILS:
• They're killer eruptions because they shoot out boiling clouds of ash, gas and rock called pyroclastic flows (see page 30).
• Pyroclastic flows rush downhill at speeds of up to 200 km/h, destroying everything in their path.
• The thick, pasty lava often builds up lava domes.

DANGER RATING: Extreme

5 PLINIAN

NAMED AFTER: Pliny the Younger

DEADLY DETAILS:
- They're the most violent eruptions. Magma rich in bubbles of gas rises very quickly and explodes with a mind-boggling bang.
- They shoot out colossal columns of ash and gas up to 45 km high. The ash can fall for hundreds of kilometres around.
- They're named after Pliny the Younger, a Roman writer who witnessed the (Plinian) eruption of Mount Vesuvius in Italy in AD 79.

DANGER RATING: Extreme

COULD YOU BE A VULCANOLOGIST?

How sparky is your volcanic know-how?
Find out with this fiery quiz.

1 How many active volcanoes are there
on Earth?
a) 500
b) 5 million
c) 1,500

2 Which country's got the most volcanoes?
a) USA
b) Japan
c) Indonesia

3 Which is the oldest volcano?
a) Etna
b) Vesuvius
c) Merapi

4 Which is the youngest volcano?
a) Eldfell
b) Surtsey
c) Paricutin

5 Which is the biggest volcano?
a) Mount St Helens
b) Mauna Loa
c) Pinatubo

6 Which is the most active volcano?
a) Kilauea
b) Mauna Loa
c) Stromboli

Answers:

1 c) There are at least 1,500 active volcanoes on Earth and about 50–60 of them erupt every year. Millions more smoulder away underneath the sea. Three quarters of the world's volcanoes lie in a circle around the Pacific Ocean, called the 'Ring of Fire'. Here the sea-floor crust is being dragged under the land, with explosive results.

2 c) It's official! Indonesia's the most explosive country on Earth, boasting more than 70 active volcanoes. They include some of the vilest volcanoes ever, such as Krakatoa and Tambora (see pages 57-66). (By the way, Japan's in second place with the USA a well-earned third.)

3 a) Volcanoes have been around for a horribly long time. They first erupted on the brand-new Earth when it formed about 4,600 million years ago. But vulcanologists reckon most of the active volcanoes around today are less than 100,000 years old. So it's congratulations to Mount Etna in Italy for reaching the grand old age of 350,000! This makes it one of the oldest volcanoes on Earth.

4 a) At a paltry 35 years old, Eldfell on the island of Heimaey in Iceland is a real youngster in volcanic terms. It appeared early in the morning of 23 January 1973 when a creeping crack almost 2 kilometres long suddenly appeared on the edge of the main town. Within two months, the erupting

Earth had built a cinder cone more than 200 metres tall. The horrified locals called this freaky peak Eldfell, which means 'fire mountain'.

5 b) Mauna Loa on the island of Hawaii is the biggest active volcano and also the largest mountain on Earth. From its bottom on the seabed, it measures a monster 9 kilometres, even taller than Mount Everest. Only the shield-shaped top of the  volcano pokes above the water but even that's a tremendous 4 kilometres tall. This vast volcano last erupted in 1984 but that was the 39th time in the last 150 years.

6 a) Another Hawaiian volcano, Kilauea, began erupting in 1983 and it's been puffing away ever since. That's the longest eruption in history. It spurts out slow-moving lava flows that have smothered parts of the island but added another square kilometre to the coast. Runner-up Stromboli, in Italy, has been erupting for at least 2,500 years. That's quite a bit longer but it has had lots of refreshing rests in between.

HOW TO MAKE A VOLCANO

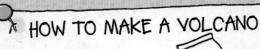

WHAT YOU NEED:
- A plastic drink bottle
- 6 mugs of flour
- 2 mugs of salt
- 6 tablespoons of cooking oil
- Some warm water
- 3 tablespoons of baking soda
- 8 drops of washing-up liquid
- Red food colouring
- Bottle of vinegar
- A grown-up to help you

WHAT YOU DO:

1 Put the flour, salt and oil in a bowl and mix until you get a thick dough.

2 Stand the bottle on a tray. Press the dough around it to make a conical volcano shape.

3 Paint the volcano and leave it to dry.

4 Pour the warm water into the bottle until it's nearly full.

5 Add the washing-up liquid, baking soda and food colouring.

6 Slowly pour the vinegar in the bottle, and stand back to watch the volcano erupt!

VILE VOLCANO VISITING

If you're dead set on visiting a volcano, read this chapter before you leave home. It could save your life. Volcano visiting can be horribly thrilling but it's also horribly difficult and dangerous. The good news is: not all volcanoes are violent killers. The bad news is: a few of them could seriously damage your health. And with around 50 volcanoes erupting each year, it pays to know which sort you're up against. So, to help you plan your trip and get back in one piece, this chapter's packed with essential survival tips. But first, you need to find out if you've got what it takes to take on a vile volcano … and win.

Could you be a vulcanologist?

Q 1: What is a vulcanologist?

A: A vulcanologist's a scientist who studies volcanoes.

Q 2: What does a vulcanologist do?

A: Vulcanologists monitor volcanoes with loads of high-tech equipment (see page 75) to try to work out how and when they're going to erupt next. If the vulcanologists spot any warning signs, they can tell people living nearby to get outta the way ... fast.

Q 3: Where does a vulcanologist work?

A: A lot of a vulcanologist's time is spent travelling around the world and visiting real-life volcanoes. Some of these peaks are horribly high so you'll need to be physically fit.

Q 4: What if you don't like heights?

A: Back home, you can do vital work in the lab like looking at volcanic gas and rock samples, and computer modelling. That means setting up computer programmes that can predict how magma might rise and how far lava might flow if a vile volcano blows. This is horribly useful for studying what goes on inside the volcano without having to get too close.

Q 5: Hmm. Any other lab work I could stuck into?

A: Yes, but you'll need to be feeling brave. Some volcanologists have built a machine in their lab which breaks volcanic rocks apart ... at the same high temperatures and pressures found inside a volcano. No wonder this smashing machine's in a room with seriously thick, steel walls. It lets them measure the strength of lava and even monitor the creaking and groaning of the rocks just before they blast apart.

Q 6: How can I become a vulcanologist?

A: For a start, you'll need to be horribly good at geography and science. Sorry. At university, most vulcanologists study something like geography, geology or geophysics. You'll get more hands-on training on the job.

Q 7: What else do I need to be good at?

A: You'll need to be able to work long hours (including evenings and weekends) and leave home at short notice if a volcano looks likely to blow. You'll also need to be good with computers and at writing reports about your findings. Being a red-hot photographer's dead handy for impressing your friends afterwards.

Q 8: Gulp! Anything else?

A: Oh, and it helps to be horribly hardy. This is no job for wimps.

SURVIVAL TIP

What do a kazen, lua pele, and gunung api have in common? Sounds like a load of gobbledygook but they're actually all words for volcanoes. If you're going to be a volcanic globetrotter, you need to know what on Earth you're talking about. (By the way, you'll find a kazen in Japan, a lua pele in Hawaii, and a gunung api in Indonesia. In case you were wondering.)

Top five horrible volcanic hazards (to avoid)

A*)* Lethal lava flows
What they are: Lava that erupts and flows down a volcano's sides.
Dangerous details:

Lava can reach a scorching 1,250°C – that's seriously hot. But it usually only chugs along at walking pace so you've got plenty of time to get out of its way. Trouble is, once a lava flow gets going, it's horribly hard to stop. It buries cars, roads, houses and even whole

towns, or sets them on fire. The fastest flow gushed out of a lake on Nyiragongo volcano in Zaire in 1977. It sped along at a staggering 100 km/h, killing hundreds of people in its path.

B) Appalling ash clouds

What they are: Vast clouds of volcanic ash blasted into the air.

Dangerous details:

Violent volcanoes chuck out millions of tonnes of awesome ash. Some of it stays in the atmosphere where it can block out the sun and change the

weather around the world (see page 65). Some of it falls back to the ground, smothering homes, towns and farmers' fields, bringing down power lines, and making it horribly hard to breathe. In 2010, ash from the tongue-twisting Eyjafjallajoekull volcano in Iceland caused chaos across Europe, grounding flights and leaving passengers stranded.

HORRIBLE HEALTH WARNING

What's the best way of avoiding an ash cloud? Not by hopping on a plane, that's for sure. Ash clogs up its engines, causing serious damage. In 1989, a Boeing 747 flew into a choking ash cloud from Redoubt volcano in Alaska. Suddenly, all four engines shut down. For 12 heart-stopping minutes, the plane glided downwards until the crew managed to restart the engines and make a safe landing. It had been a truly terrifying ride.

C) Ghastly gases

What they are: Gases, like carbon dioxide and sulphur dioxide, that volcanoes belch out.

Dangerous details:

The vilest volcanic gas is killer carbon dioxide. It doesn't smell of anything so you don't even know it's there. But breathe too much of it in and you'll be dead in 10 minutes or less. In 1986, a cloud of deadly carbon dioxide leaked from Lake Nyos in Cameroon. The lake lay in a volcanic crater and, over hundreds of years, the gases had seeped up from deep under the ground. On that dreadful night, the ghastly gas poured silently and unseen down the valley, suffocating every living thing in its path.

D) Loathsome lahars

What they are: Massive mudflows made when volcanic ash mixes with water.

Dangerous details:

Lahars hurtle down a volcano at speeds of up to 160 km/h. They can flow for hundreds of kilometres before coming to a halt. Then the murderous mud sets hard, like concrete. On its perilous path, it buries people, buildings and fields, and clogs up rivers. Worse still, long-dead lahars can suddenly come back to life. When Mount Pinatubo in the Philippines erupted in 1991, lahars devastated the local landscape. Three years later, heavy monsoon rains caused the murderous mud to start flowing again.

E) Fatal pyroclastic flows

What they are: Boiling, billowing clouds of ash, gas and rock.

Deadly details:

Stand in the path of a fatal flow and you'll be sorry. Dead sorry. They're the deadliest of all volcanic hazards. These killers stream down a volcano's sides like awful

avalanches, hugging the ground for several kilometres. They can flow across water without even slowing down. They're super speedy – racing along at up to 200 km/h, that's faster than an express train; red-hot – up to 800°C; and absolutely lethal – victims die from breathing in hot ash and gas, and from being buried. When Mont Pelee erupted in 1902, a fatal pyroclastic flow demolished the city of St Pierre and killed 28,000 people.

HORRIBLE HEALTH WARNING

Apart from all the other stuff a volcano coughs up, there's another horrible hazard to watch out for. Lightning often strikes when a volcano erupts – one vulcanologist counted 300 strikes in just 10 minutes – and it can be lethal. Worse still, with not many trees around to take the strain, you're likely to be the tallest thing about...

Ten killer volcanoes

Date	Volcano	Deaths	Major cause of death
1815	Tambora, Indonesia	92,000	Starvation after the eruption
1883	Krakatau, Indonesia	36,500	Tsunami
1902	Mont Pelee, Martinique	29,000	Pyroclastic flows
1985	Nevado del Ruiz, Colombia	25,000	Lahars
1792	Mount Unzen, Japan	14,300	Lava dome collapse
1783	Laki, Iceland	9,350	Starvation after the eruption
1919	Kelut, Indonesia	5,100	Lahars
1882	Galunggung, Indonesia	4,000	Lahars
1631	Vesuvius, Italy	3,500	Lahars; lava flows
79	Vesuvius, Italy	3,350	Pyroclastic flows; Ash falls

EARTH—SHATTERING FACT

Vulcanologists use the Volcanic Explosivity Index (VEI, for short) to measure how violent a volcano is. It's based on the awesome amounts of stuff a volcano spits out. Volcanoes are graded from zero to eight and each step up means a ten-fold increase in force. So VEI 0 is horribly gentle, but get up to VEI 8 and you're talking a major catastrophe.

VEI	DESCRIPTION	VOLCANO TYPE	HOW OFTEN	EXAMPLE
0	Non explosive	Hawaiian	Daily	Kilauea
1	Gentle	Hawaiian/ Strombolian	Daily	Stromboli
2	Explosive	Strombolian/ Vulcanian	Weekly	Galeras (1992)
3	Severe	Vulcanian	Yearly	Nevado del Ruiz (1985)
4	Cataclysmic	Vulcanian/ Plinian	10s of years	Galunggung (1982)
5	Paroxysmal	Plinian	100s of years	Mount St Helens (1980)
6	Colossal	Plinian/ Ultra-Plinian	100s of years	Krakatau (1883)
7	Super-colossal	Ultra-Plinian	1000s of years	Tambora (1815)
8	Mega-colossal	Ultra-Plinian	10,000s of years	Yellowstone (2 mya)

VOLCANO SAFETY GUIDE

1 DO get to know your volcano
Before you set off. Find out if it's active or when it last went up. Is it monitored regularly? And are warnings likely to be given if it starts to erupt?

2 DO dress the part
It could be a matter of life or death. You'll need:

• A climbing helmet or hard hat: to protect your head from falling rocks.

• A gas mask: so you don't breathe in toxic fumes and ash.

• Leather gloves: to stop your hands being cut or burned by lava.

• Sturdy boots: solidified lava can be sharp and can cut shoes to shreds.

• Goggles: to protect your eyes from ash and dust.

• Long trousers and long-sleeved top: to save your skin if you fall.

WRONG   RIGHT

3 DON'T walk on lava flows

However slow and sluggish they look. As lava cools, it turns into hard rock but it can still be red-hot and runny underneath. (A flow can take a year to cool down completely.) If the shelly crust suddenly goes crack, you'll fall in and be fried or badly cut. Keep close to the edge and listen out for crunching noises as you walk.

4 DO steer clear of lava bombs

Volcanoes, even gentle ones, can chuck out whopping chunks of flying rock. Watch where these bombs are landing and keep well out of the way. If a bomb's coming towards you, don't run away. Hold on to your hard hat, stay calm and dodge to one side at the last minute. Then shelter behind a big boulder, and cover your head with your rucksack.

5 DON'T breathe in toxic fumes

Always wear your gas mask or tie a damp cloth over your nose and mouth. (Some vulcanologists reckon a cloth soaked in wee works best. Honestly.) Some gases have a strong smell so are easy to detect (hydrogen sulphide reeks of rotten eggs) but others don't pong at all. Even if the fumes don't kill you, you'll feel horribly dizzy and sick.

6 DO watch out for rock falls

Climbing a volcano can be risky. Always wear your helmet to protect your head from falling rocks. And watch where you're putting your feet. Try not to kick loose rocks down – there might be other climbers below. Be extra careful around the crater where the newly cooled lava might be cracking up.

7 DO check out the risk zones

Zone 1: Extreme risk (around the vent):
Get caught in an eruption here and you've got 30 seconds to escape. MAXIMUM.

Zone 2: High risk (100 metres–300 metres):
The edge of the crater. You've a 50:50 chance of surviving here.

Zone 3: Medium risk (300 metres–3 km):
Safer but you're still at risk of being bashed by flying rocks and ash.

Zone 4: Low risk (3 km–10 km):
Usually safe but look out for lava flows, lahars and pyroclastic flows.

Zone 5: Safe zone (beyond 10 km):
Safe for people to live in, although lahars from violent eruptions can still reach this far.

Note: Where the zones stop and start depends on which volcano you're on so check it out before you get too close.

8 DO plan an escape route

Volcanoes are horribly fickle. Even a seemingly safe volcano can suddenly erupt. Keep a map of the local area handy and have an escape route planned. Better still; take a local guide who'll know the quickest and safest way down.

VILE VOLCANO 1: MOUNT ST HELENS

It is 18 May 1980 in the Cascade Range of mountains in the northwestern USA. For everybody watching, this will be a day they will never forget. For months, vulcanologists have been monitoring the picture-postcard-but-perilous peak of Mount St Helens. All the warning signs point to an earth-shattering eruption but no one is ready for what happens next. Mount St Helens has been slumbering peacefully for 123 years but it seems now that this sleeping giant is picking up steam. At just after 8.30 am, a massive earthquake shakes the mountain. Then, suddenly and with staggering force, this vile volcano blows itself to smithereens. Time to meet Mount St Helens…

WELCOME TO MT ST HELENS

...OME TO M...ELENS

BEFORE

AFTER

VILE VOLCANO FACT FILE

Name: **Mount St Helens**
Location: **Washington State, USA**
Type: **Stratovolcano**
Last major eruption: **1980 (VEI 5)**
Height (before 1980 eruption): **2,950 metres**
Height (after 1980 eruption): **2,550 metres**
Last eruption: **2008**
Status: **Active**

NORTH AMERICA

Mount St Helens facts
- Mount St Helens is one of 15 active volcanoes in the Cascade Range.
- Here, one plate of the Earth's crust's being dragged under another ... with explosive results.
- At a paltry 40,000 years old, Mount St Helens is still a vile volcano youngster.
- Native Americans believe the peak is a beautiful princess who was turned to stone.

Mount St Helens: Volcano visitor's guide

- **Getting there:**

Hitch a lift on a helicopter or light plane. It's the best way to see the crater and lava dome and you won't even get out of breath. Or you can climb to the summit, if you're feeling fit. It's a round trip of 7–12 hours and the going's quite rocky and tough. Don't forget your permit. Only 100 people are allowed to climb the mountain every day.

- **Where to stay:**

Fancy camping? There are plenty of campsites in Mount St Helens National Monument (national park) and you'll get a brilliant view. If you're a vulcanologist, you can even camp in the crater.

- **What to take:**

You don't need any special equipment in summer. But in winter, you'd need some serious gear like ice-axes, crampons and ropes. A good map or guidebook's a must-have, and a camera for taking a snap at the top.

- **When to go:**

The best time to go is mid-June to late September when you'll get long, sunny days and clear views.

- **Other places to visit:**

Mount Rainier: It last erupted in 1894 but it's still active. And it's horribly dangerous because it's so close to several busy cities. If this beauty went up in smoke, millions of people would be at risk of flooding as the 26 glaciers on its summit melted.

Crater Lake: It's a beautifully blue, crystal-clear lake lying in an ancient volcanic crater. The crater was blasted out when Mount Mazama erupted about 7,000 years ago. Watch out for Wizard Island. It's a steep-sided cinder cone you might just mistake for a wizard's hat.

DIARY OF A DISASTER

Before...

In March 1980, vulcanologists monitoring Mount St Helens recorded a series of small but shocking earthquakes. Days later, the quakes were coming thicker and faster, and a loud explosion was heard. Mount St Helens was stirring. A plane circling the summit reported colossal cracks in the glaciers and an awesome column of ash and steam. Soon, sightseers were flocking to watch the fireworks, and locals set up stalls selling souvenirs like 'I Lava Volcano' T-shirts. For safety, an exclusion zone was set up around the mountain but many people ignored it to get a better look.

As April passed, the north side of the mountain began bulging ominously as magma from deep inside the Earth started muscling its way upward. Alarmingly, by mid-May, the bulge was more than 100 metres high ... and still growing. Something would have to give.

During...

At 8.32 am on 18 May, an enormous and earth-shattering earthquake shook Mount St Helens. What happened next took everyone by surprise. The whole north side of the mountain collapsed, sending a staggering 6 billion tonnes of rock racing downhill. It was the largest landslide in history but the volcano wasn't spent yet.

The landslide relieved the pressure on the magma inside, but with disastrous results… Suddenly, the blister-like bulge blew apart, blasting out a pyroclastic flow of hot gas, ash and rock. The fatal flow raced along the ground at speeds of 500 km/h, snapping millions of trees like puny matchsticks. It was so horrendously hot, it even melted the sap inside. To make matters worse, the heat from the blast melted the glaciers on the mountain's summit. Meltwater mixed with ash to form massive mudflows that slithered down the slopes, clogging up the region's once-raging rivers.

Meanwhile, the super-sized slide of rock and ice slammed into Spirit Lake, 8 kilometres away. It dumped so much debris into the lake, the water level rose by 60 metres. Then it hurtled towards the Toutle River, sweeping away people, bridges and homes.

After…

In the space of a few fateful minutes, the landscape around Mount St Helens was changed for ever. The mountain's once-perfect cone was replaced with a gaping crater, shaped like a giant horseshoe. Fabulous forests, sparkling lakes and rushing rivers – once popular spots with holiday-makers – lay buried under ghastly grey ash. Further afield, millions more tonnes of ash, blown by the wind, fell to Earth like dirty, grey snow over towns and fields.

GIANT HORSESHOE

The earth-shattering eruption of Mount St Helens was the deadliest in US history. Tragically, 57 people died, mostly well outside the exclusion zone. The main eruption lasted for another nine nerve-wracking hours then, finally, began to die down. Smaller eruptions followed, off and on, for the next six years, building a brand-new lava dome in the collapsed crater.

EARTH—SHATTERING FACT

After the eruption, the landscape around Mount St Helens looked like something from the Moon. But, incredibly, when the dust settled, it began coming back to life. Thanks to the freezing cold weather, some plucky plants and animals had survived the blast. Plants were protected underneath thick snow. Fish were found alive in lakes covered by ice. And small animals, like mice and gophers, had dug themselves into snug burrows underground.

DID I MISS ANYTHING?

Answers:
Incredibly, they're all TRUE! Ignore them if you dare…

1 True. Earthquakes are a common sign a vile volcano's about to blow. And as the eruption gets closer, the earthquakes come thicker and faster. They're a sure sign that magma underground is starting to stir.

2 True. Watch out for unusual bumps and bulges in the mountainside. As magma wells up, it makes the sides of the mountain swell. Just before Mount St Helens erupted, vulcanologists noticed the bulge on its north side was growing at around 2 metres a day.

3 True. Volcanoes are horribly noisy so keep your ear to the ground. They whoosh, whine and rumble, and also hiss, roar and splutter. They even chug like a train. You'll also hear sounds like gunshots but they're really small explosions.

4 True. As magma reaches the surface, it gives off ghastly gases that seep up through cracks in the ground. So if you smell rotten eggs, it's actually hydrogen sulphide gas and it's not to be sniffed at. See page 29 for other ghastly gases to avoid.

5 True. Surprisingly, vulcanologists have found that the tallest, greenest plants on a volcano sprout in places where magma's most likely to spurt out. So it's not the time to stop and do a spot of gardening.

Four shocking survivors' stories

On the morning of 18 May, Jim Scymanky and three others were cutting wood about 20 kilometres away, out of sight of the mountain. Looking up, they spotted the blast cloud racing towards them. The force knocked Scymanky down and melted his gloves to his hands. When he came to, he was horribly badly burned but lucky to be alive.

Geologists, Keith and Dorothy Stoeffel, were flying above Mount St Helens in a small plane and witnessed the north side of the mountain collapsing. Seconds later came the blast cloud that threatened to engulf their plane, somehow, the pilot managed to outrun it by heading south. Any other direction would have meant certain death.

Twenty-two kilometres away, Bruce Nelson, Sue Ruff and two friends had pitched camp on the bank of the Green River. They were a safe distance from the volcano. Surely? Then, without warning, the blast cloud blew in… In the ashy darkness, Nelson and Ruff accidentally fell into a hole left by a blown-down tree. The temperature in the hole reached a scorching 300°F, hot enough to singe their hair. They survived their terrifying ordeal but their friends were killed by falling trees.

Venus Dergan and Ronald Reitan were camping by the Toutle River when the water rose and swept them away in a sea of logs. For a while, they clung to the roof of their car but were later thrown off. Dergan was sucked under but Reitan pulled her up again by her hair. They finally escaped by wading through knee-deep muddy water to a road and climbing up a steep hill.

EARTH—SHATTERING FACT

In April 2008, American John Slemp, had a very lucky escape. While riding his snowmobile on Mount St Helens, Slemp plunged 500 metres into the snow-filled crater. Slemp kept warm by huddling over a gushing fountain of steam until he was eventually rescued by helicopter. Despite his awful ordeal, he only suffered minor injuries.

VILE VOLCANO 2: KILAUEA

For the chance to watch a volcano close up without being blown up or fried, head for heavenly Hawaii in the Pacific Ocean. These flaming islands are the tops of vast volcanoes towering up from the seabed. Horrible geographers call them hot-spot volcanoes because of the way they grow (check out the inside story on page 50). Head straight for the biggest island, confusingly named Hawaii (though locals call it 'Big Island'). If you can stand the heat... The island's actually built from five vile volcanoes so there's plenty for you to gawp at. But watch your step. These freaky peaks are famous for oozing out oodles of lively lava so it can get horribly hot underfoot.

HOTFOOT IT TO HAWAII

VILE VOLCANO FACT FILE

Name: **Kilauea**, Location: **Hawaii**
Type: **Shield volcano**
Height: **1,277 metres**
Last major eruption: **From 1983 to present day (VEI 1)**
Status: **Active**

Kilauea facts

● Kilauea's the most active volcano on the planet. It has erupted non-stop since 1983 and is still going strong.

● Its name means 'spreading' or 'spewing' and no wonder. It spews out some 500,000 cubic metres of lava (that's enough to fill 200 Olympic swimming pools) EVERY DAY.

● In fact, it has oozed out so much lava, it has added 300 soccer pitches' worth of land to the island.

Kilauea: Volcano visitor's guide

• Getting there:

Hire a car and drive right around the rim of the crater along cunningly named Crater Rim Drive. But watch out – bits of the road have been buried by fresh lava. Or you can hike up Crater Rim Trail if you fancy a walk and you've got all day. Oddly, you'll hike through a blooming rainforest before you reach the rocky, lava landscape.

• Where to stay:

Check into the Volcano House Hotel and ask for a crater-side view. Then toast yourself by the lava fireplace before sipping a flaming cocktail.

• What to take:

Wear sturdy boots, otherwise the lava will cut your feet to shreds. You'll also need to drink plenty of water – hiking over lava's thirsty work. Take a torch if you're walking back in the dark. It's horribly easy to get lost.

• When to go:

Sunset's a spectacular time to watch the lava show. But the crater gets horribly crowded so you might be better off getting up early and going at dawn.

• Other places to visit:

Mauna Loa: You can't miss Mauna Loa – it's the biggest volcano and also the most massive mountain on Earth. This vile volcano last erupted in 1984 and it's being carefully monitored for more signs of life.

Mauna Kea: Visit Mauna Kea's awesome astronomical observatory for a glittering glimpse of the stars. It'll leave you starry-eyed. You'll get the best view at midnight but wrap up warm, especially in winter when this parky peak's covered in snow.

HORRIBLE HEALTH WARNING

Since it started erupting, busy Kilauea's been belching out a breathtaking 1,000 tonnes of odious sulphur dioxide EVERY DAY. That's an awful lot of gas. Trouble is, it mixes with chemicals in the air to make a vile volcanic smog called vog. Vog's vicious. It can sting your eyes and make it hard to breathe. It gets worse in the afternoon so avoid being out and about after lunch.

Hot-spot volcanoes

The idyllic islands of Hawaii are called hot–spot volcanoes and here are the highlights of how they grow…

a) A fountain of magma rises up from deep in the Earth's mantle, close to the core…

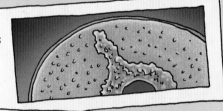

b) …and punches a hole in the sea bed crust to form a hot spot.

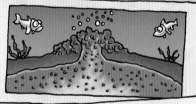

c) Magma bubbles up through the hole and turns into solid rock.

d) The rock builds up and up, forming a vile volcano.

e) Eventually, it grows big enough to poke up as an island (though this takes millions and millions of years).

f) Over the years, the hot spot stays rooted to the spot while the plate above drifts slowly across it.

g) As it does so, the magma punches new holes in the seabed and brand-new volcanoes are born.

EARTH—SHATTERING FACT

As the volcanoes shift away from the hot spot, they cool down and die. But it's not all doom and gloom because new ones pop up to take their place. A new Hawaiian volcano called Loihi's busy bubbling away under the sea and it's already almost 3 kilometres tall. But if you fancy paying it a visit, you're in for a very long wait. It's still a whole kilometre underwater and won't break the surface for at least another 60,000 years.

Could you be a vulcanologist?

You might think all lava looks the same. But you'd be wrong. Lava comes in lots of different kinds, all with lava-ly sounding names. But which ones do you reckon are real?

Answers:
Apart from number 8, the answer to all of them is…YES!

1 Yes. It billows out of cracks in the seabed, cools very quickly when it hits the water and solidifies into large, lumpy blobs. Some 'pillows' can measure 7 metres across so you'd need a whopping bed.

2 Yes. But you wouldn't want to brush your teeth with it. It's seriously thick and sticky, and gets squeezed out through cracks in the lava crust.

3 Yes. It's the Hawaiian word for lava that's thick and gloopy, and forms sharp, jagged rock when it cools. You pronounce the word 'ah-ah', the sound you'd make if you walked over it.

4 Yes. It's a round blob of lava chucked out of a volcano and it looks just like a splat of cow poo. You also get chunks of lava that look like pancakes, ribbons and loaves of bread.

THAT'S NOT MINE!

5 Yes. It's pronounced 'pa–hoy–hoy', and it's another bit of volcanic Hawaiian vocab. It's gooey, runny lava that looks like huge coils of rope when it goes cold.

6 Yes. It's an egg-shaped lump of lava about the size of a baseball. From the outside, it looks like a boring old rock but inside, it's filled with sparkling crystals. People used to think thunder eggs dropped from the sky during thunderstorms.

7 Yes. Pele's the Hawaiian fire goddess who's believed to live inside Kilauea. Fine, glassy strands of lava blown out of the volcano are known as Pele's hair.

8 No. A bocca's actually a name for the volcano's vent and that's where lava spurts out. The word means 'mouth' in Italian.

SURVIVAL TIP

If you fancy putting your feet up, don't be tempted to sit down on a lava bench. It's where a lava flow pours into the sea. For a start, the lava's still roasting hot and instantly transforms the sea into scalding steam And it's horribly unstable, so it could suddenly collapse and hurl you into the sizzling sea.

Five ways of stopping a lava flow

A) DAM IT

In 1960, a lava flow from Kilauea was spotted heading straight towards the village of Kapoho. Quick-thinking villagers built six huge earth barriers to stop the loathsome lava in its tracks. Sadly, the lava dribbled over the top and the village was  history. It was a different story on Mount Etna in Italy when it erupted in 1983. Four whopping rock-and-earth barriers were strong enough to save several important buildings, including an astronomical observatory.

- Success rating: 5/10

B) BLAST IT

Another explosive idea for diverting lava was to drop bombs on it. This was tried out in 1935 when a lava tube from Mauna Loa was blasted apart to stop it reaching the town of Hilo. And it worked. Well, sort of. It's true the lava trickled to  a halt outside the town but the eruption had stopped anyway. In 1992, the same idea was used on Mount Etna in Operation Volcano Buster. This time concrete blocks were also dropped into the hole.

- Success rating: 6/10

C) DIG IT

The first people known to have a go at halting a lava flow were 50 locals living near Mount Etna. In 1669, lava erupted on the south side and headed straight towards the seaside town

of Catania. Armed with picks and shovels, the men set to work hacking the flow apart. The good news was: the lava changed course and Catania was safe ... for now. The bad news was: another town was now in danger! A royal decree was passed forbidding anyone from going anywhere near the flow.

- Success rating: 3/10

D) SPRAY IT

In 1973, the islanders of Heimaey in Iceland watched in horror as lava from a newly erupting volcano flowed fatefully towards the harbour. Without the harbour, the fishing industry would be lost, and with it, the islanders' livelihoods.

COOL!

Then someone had a cunning but crackpot idea. They'd spray the lava with seawater to cool it down so it turned into solid rock and stopped. Astonishingly, their potty plan worked! OK, so it took five hard months of hosing and used billions and billions of litres of water. But the lava stopped short of the harbour, so who's counting?

- Success rating: 8/10

E) Pray to it

According to Hawaiian beliefs, the hot-tempered goddess Pele only has to stamp her feet and Kilauea erupts. So it's vital to keep her happy by throwing offerings into the crater. Take your pick from flowers, sweets and breadfruit or even pigs,

ER, GUYS, I DON'T THINK THIS IS GOING TO WORK!

brandy and human hair. If Mount Vesuvius in Italy looks like erupting, locals call on St Januarius for help. He's the patron saint of Naples and his saintly skull is kept in a nearby chapel (his head was chopped off by the Romans). When Vesuvius starts stirring, the saintly skull's brought out and paraded in front of the volcano to quieten it down.

● Success rating: 1/10

VILE VOLCANO 3: KRAKATAU

Next stop on your vile volcanic tour's the wild islands of Indonesia. So you'll need to be feeling brave. Because of its position above two pushy plates, it's one of the most explosive places on Earth. Around 130 active volcanoes bubble away, with some ten or so eruptions every year. Having second thoughts? It's not surprising. The volcano you're about to visit's called Krakatau and it's a mind-blowing blast from the past. It lies in the Indian Ocean between Java and Sumatra and for centuries, people thought it was extinct. Then, in August 1883, this vile volcanic island suddenly turned violent and blew itself apart. Read on for the earth-shattering details…

KRAKATAU: A CRACKING VOLCANO!

VILE VOLCANO FACT FILE

Name: **Krakatau**
Location: **Sunda Strait, Indonesia**
Type: **Stratovolcano**
Last major eruption: **1883 (VEI 6)**
Height (before 1883 eruption): **813 metres**
Area (before 1883 eruption): **34 sq km**
Area (after 1883 eruption): **11 sq km**
Last eruption: **2007/2008**
Status: **Active**

Krakatau facts

● Before 1883, Krakatau island was made of three volcanoes – Rataka, Danan and Perbuwatan.
● Two-thirds of the island slumped into the sea, leaving only half of Rataka above water.
● The eruption blasted a colossal 30 cubic kilometres of rock and ash 80 km into the air.

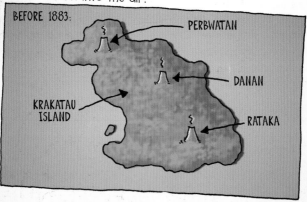

BEFORE 1883:

PERBWATAN

DANAN

KRAKATAU ISLAND

RATAKA

● The sound of the eruption was the loudest ever heard. It reached as far as Rodrigues Island almost 5,000 km away in the Indian Ocean where people mistook it for gunfire.

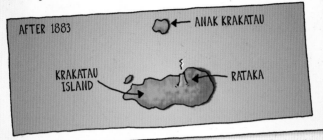

AFTER 1883

ANAK KRAKATAU

KRAKATAU ISLAND

RATAKA

HORRIBLE HEALTH WARNING

In December 1927, local fishermen were shocked to see smoke and steam belching from the sea where Krakatau had once stood. Over the next three years, a brand-new cinder cone volcano began bubbling up and today it's more than 300 metres tall. It's called Anak Krakatau which means 'child of Krakatau', though there's nothing sweet and cuddly about this earth-shattering island.

DOESN'T LOOK LIKE A VERY HAPPY CHILD!

Anak Krakatau: Volcano visitor's guide

- **Getting there:**

Take a boat from the west coast of Java around 50 km away. It takes about five hours. But be warned. The sea can be horribly choppy so you'll soon be turning a nice shade of green.

- **Where to stay:**

If the weather's fine, you can get there and back in a day. Otherwise, you can camp on nearby Rataka, the only bit left of the original island.

- **What to take:**

Anak Krakatau and Rataka are deserted so you'll need to pack everything you need – water, food, tents and warm clothes. They'll also be handy if your boat goes adrift. And a local guide's a must.

- **When to go:**

Anak Krakatau may be small but it's horribly dangerous. If the volcano's quiet, you can scramble up to the crater but watch out for loose rubble and rocks. If it's erupting, you have to keep your distance and stay 3 kilometres away from its perilous peak. Otherwise, you could be toast.

- **Other places to visit:**

Merapi (Java): It's a lava dome and the most active volcano in Indonesia, erupting almost all of the time. No wonder its name means 'Fire Mountain' in the local language. Despite the dangers, half a million of people live nearby in the crowded city of Yogyakarta.

Galunggung (Java): It's another active volcano so you'll need to watch your step. Especially if you're wandering about the Ten Thousand Hills. They're thousands of bumpy hummocks, formed from lumps of rock and ash dumped by an eruption long ago.

Eruption countdown

Early May 1883
Several small earthquakes shake the region. But quakes are so common in Indonesia, no one takes much notice.

20 May 1883
A ship's captain reports seeing ash and steam belching from Krakatau. The sound of explosions can be heard 160 kilometres away.

22 May 1883
The fiery glow above the island can be seen from the Javan coast. Earthquakes continue throughout May and June.

20 July 1883
After a few weeks' peace and quiet, Krakatau starts erupting again. Passing ships have to dodge chunks of pumice* clogging up the sea.

(* Pumice is a kind of volcanic rock, usually formed in the most explosive eruptions. It's full of holes left by gas bubbles and these make it light enough to float.)

26 August 1883

At around 1 pm, Krakatau exploded with a roar that blasts a black cloud of ash and rock almost 25 kilometres into the air. Throughout the day, the eruption gets more violent. But worse is yet to come…

27 August 1883

Between 5.30 am and 11 am, four gigantic explosions rip Krakatau apart. Two-thirds of the island collapses and sinks under the waves. Around a thousand people are killed by fearsome pyroclastic flows and scorching ash. But tens of thousands more are drowned when killer tsunamis (see page 64) come crashing down on to nearby coasts.

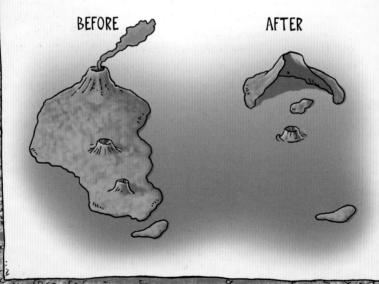

BEFORE   AFTER

An explosive story

As the eruption reached its peak, people along the nearby coasts began to fear for their lives. Here's how one elderly local described the dreadful scene…

Anyer, west coast of Java, August 1883
"The eruption began on Sunday afternoon (26 August). We did not take much notice at first until the explosions grew very loud. Then we noticed that Krakatau was completely enveloped in smoke. Afterwards came the thick darkness, so black and intense that I could not see my hand before my eyes…Towards night, everything became worse. The noise was deafening, and a red fiery glare was visible in the sky above the burning mountain. Although Krakatau was 40 kilometres away … many of the houses shook so much that we feared every minute would bring them down. There was little sleep for any of us that dreadful night. Before daybreak on Monday, on going out of doors, I found the showers of ashes had begun, and this gradually increased in force until at length large pieces of pumice-stone kept falling around."

EARTH–SHATTERING FACT

For months afterwards, the sea around Krakatau was choked with chunks of pumice the size of cars. And it was horribly useful. Believe it or not. Three years later, surprised scientists counted 26 different kinds of plants sprouting happily on what was left of the island, even though the island's original bloomers had perished in the blast. It seemed the seeds they grew from had been carried by the wind, in birds' droppings and on the pumice rafts.

JUST DOING MY BIT!

Could you be a vulcanologist?

Serious about visiting volcanoes? Sure you can stand the heat? You might like to stick to collecting stamps when you've read about some of the sinister side effects.

1 Tsunamis
A tsunami (soo–nar–mee) is a series of whopping waves triggered by deep–sea earthquakes … or volcanoes. The collapse of Krakatau into the sea set off tsunamis up to 40 metres high. These killer waves smashed ashore, washing away 165 villages along nearby coasts and drowning some 36,000 people.

2 Cool weather

Violent volcanoes can belch out so much awful ash and gas (sulphur dioxide's particularly to blame), it blots out the sun. This can change weather patterns around the world. When Mount Tambora in Indonesia erupted in 1815, temperatures in the northern half the world fell by up to 3°C. In North America, 1816 became known as 'the year without summer' and snow even fell in June.

3 Crop failure

After the eruption of Tambora, the ash killed crops on nearby islands and tens of thousands of people starved to death. But the shock was felt much further afield. Crops failed in many parts of Europe, leading to fatal famine and disease. There were outbreaks of looting and rioting, and in some places, famished people were reduced to eating rats.

4 Red skies at night

Sunlight filtering through volcanic ash creates spectacular special effects. For three years after Krakatau blew, sunsets were so brilliant some people mistook them for fires and called out the fire brigade. There were also reports of haloes appearing around the moon, and of the sun turning a sinister shade of green or blue.

EARTH-SHATTERING FACT

If you thought Krakatua and Tambora were earth shattering enough, thank your lucky stars you weren't around 75,000 years ago. When Mount Toba (also in Indonesia) went and blew its top, scientists reckon that the eruption would have measured a mind-boggling VEI 8. Terrible Toba spewed out so much ash, horrible humans were almost wiped out and the planet was plunged into a freezing-cold winter that lasted for year after bone-chilling year

VILE VOLCANO 4: VESUVIUS

Italy's famous for the ancient Romans, fabulous food and sensational scenery. And ... violent volcanoes. Three of them – Vesuvius, Etna and Stromboli – are particularly perilous. To visit Etna and Stromboli, you'll have to head to the islands of Sicily and, er, Stromboli, off the coast. But first, why not check out vile Vesuvius on the mainland close to the bustling city of Naples. And that's where you're heading in this chapter. You can't miss this freaky peak. It looms above the city, looking horribly harmless and picturesque. Most of the time. But don't be fooled by appearances. Vesuvius can turn nasty. Very nasty indeed.

VILE VOLCANO FACT FILE

Name: **Vesuvius**
Location: **Near Naples, Italy**
Type: **Stratovolcano**
Height: **1,281 metres**
Last major eruption: **1944 (VEI 3)**
Most famous eruption: **AD 79 (VEI 6)**
Status: **Active**

Vesuvius facts
- It's the only active volcano on mainland Europe.
- In AD 72, the gladiator Spartacus and his slave army hid from the Romans in its crater.
- The oldest volcano observatory in the world was set up on its slopes in 1845.
- The 1944 eruption destroyed two towns and 88 bomber planes at a nearby air base.

Vesuvius: Volcano visitor's guide

• Getting there:

You can drive or take the bus to the summit car park where you can stop off for a snack. Then it's a steep 1.5-km-climb to the crater, which will take you an hour at most. Afterwards, you can buy a ticket for the Vesuvius railway that runs right around the volcano's bottom.

• Where to stay:

There are plenty of hotels in nearby Naples or you could stay in San Sebastiano. The town's been destroyed by eruptions FIVE TIMES and it's a good place to have a gawp at some old lava flows.

• What to take:

No special equipment's needed but don't wear sandals, even in summer, because the ground can get horribly hot. Take some money if you want to buy a souvenir of your visit but watch out for cheating chunks of fake Vesuvius rock.

• When to go:

You can visit Vesuvius at any time of the year but it gets horribly crowded in summer. Weather-wise, the best time to go is in spring or autumn when the summit's clear of snow.

• Other places to visit:

Etna: It's one of the world's most active volcanoes so listen out for warnings before you get too close. It often erupts from cracks on its sides not just from the crater. If you're lucky, you'll see it blowing smoke rings – the only volcano with this trick up its sleeve.

Stromboli: You're sure of seeing an eruption on Stromboli – it's sizzling away most of the time. You can climb to the summit, stopping off for a pizza on the way. Or, if you're feeling lazy, you can watch the firework display on a telly screen in the nearby village.

The day a volcano blew

Pompeii, Italy, 24/25 August AD 79
In the morning of 24 August AD 79, the people of the prosperous town of Pompeii were going about their business as usual. Nobody gave Vesuvius a second thought. After all, the volcano hadn't erupted in living memory and was reckoned to be extinct. True, the ground had been shaking lately but that was because of a giant imprisoned under the mountains by the gods and struggling to break free. Surely? And then the volcano exploded with a deafening roar. The nightmare had begun.

> I WISH THIS GIANT WOULD STOP TRYING TO ESCAPE!

The volcano blasted a vast, black cloud of hot ash and pumice high in to the air. The top spread out to look like one of the umbrella-shaped pine trees that grew nearby. About half an hour later, deadly ash and pumice began falling on Pompeii, turning day into night. People fled in terror or took shelter inside buildings. By midnight, the town was buried in

a thick layer of ash. Many people were suffocated by the ash; others were killed by roofs caving in under its awesome weight. Then, the eruption cloud collapsed and things went from bad to worse… Early in the morning of 25 August, a series of boiling pyroclastic flows began roaring down the volcano's slopes, They smashed first into nearby Herculaneum and then into Pompeii, killing almost everyone who'd survived the fatal ashfalls.

The awful eruption continued for the rest of the day. Violent Vesuvius spewed out more pyroclastic flows, each one bigger and more ferocious than the one before. The final blast was accompanied by powerful earthquakes and a colossal ash cloud that turned the sky black for many kilometres around. By that time, Pompeii and Herculaneum had disappeared under many metres of deadly debris. Some 16,000 people are thought to have perished, their bodies buried under the ash.

EARTH—SHATTERING FACT

Oddly enough, the disaster that destroyed Pompeii also saved the town for posterity. The ash preserved the ruins perfectly until they were unearthed by archaeologists many centuries later. Among their grisliest discoveries were the bodies of victims who'd been suffocated by the ash. The ash set hard like a mould as the soft flesh rotted away inside. Much later, these moulds were filled with plaster of Paris to make ghostly plaster casts of the dead.

Vile volcano living quiz

Why on Earth would you live near a vile volcano? You might be surprised. But first you need to decide which of these red-hot reasons is true.

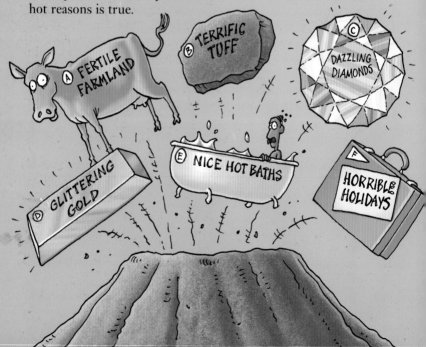

Answers:

Don't think any of them sound likely? Well, they're ALL TRUE.

a) True. You might think a vile volcano's an odd place to have a farm. And it's definitely dicey. But volcanic ash is bursting with goodness crops need to bloom. For centuries, farmers have grown grapes (for making wine) and other fruit and veg on the slopes of Vesuvius and Etna. Not

to mention rice in Indonesia, coffee in Central America, radishes in Japan, sugarcane in Hawaii and kiwi fruit in New Zealand.

b) True. Tuff's a terrifically, er, tough type of rock made from volcanic ash. And it's brilliant for sawing into building blocks. The Romans used tonnes of the stuff for building their bridges and roads. If you can't be bothered to build your own house, find yourself a tuff cliff and hollow out a cosy cave. That's what people in Turkey, Italy and other parts of the world have done for centuries. You'll soon be calling it home.

c) True. The best place to spot these sparklers is inside a volcano (check it has been extinct for a few million years first). They crop up in a type of volcanic rock called kimberlite, churned up from inside the Earth. But you'll need to dig horribly deep to

get these dreamy diamonds out. One mine in South Africa reaches a whole kilometre underground.

d) True. Hot springs spurt up in places where volcanic rocks heat up underground water and they're remarkably rich in gold – but be careful you don't get boiled. In 1992, vulcanologists were gobsmacked to find tiny globules of gold in rocks spewed out by Galeras, a vile volcano in Columbia. Delve deeper inside your volcano and you're also likely to find other marvellous metals like silver, copper, lead and zinc.

e) True. Underground water heated by hot volcanic rocks can be piped into people's homes for heating and running the bath. In Iceland, a toasty two thirds of houses are heated this way. Steam from the hot water can also be used to make electricity … or

to do some baking. Ingenious Icelandic farmers living near a volcano used steam to run a bread oven. They used to grow potatoes too, but when they dug them up the sizzling spuds were already half baked.

f) True. For a holiday that'll really blow you away, you can't beat visiting a volcano. If you're feeling energetic, head for Mount Ruapehu in New Zealand and its slippery ski slopes. But keep a look out for lahars if this vile volcano starts erupting. For something more relaxing, take a dip in a steaming mudbath in nearby Rotorua.

MY PEAS KEEP ROLLING OFF MY PLATE

Could you be a vulcanologist?

To work out if a volcano's about to erupt, vulcanologists need to keep a very close eye on it. Fancy following in their footsteps? Here are six serious bits of kit you wouldn't want to leave home without…

1 Seismometer

Function: Measuring earthquakes

How it works: It records the shock waves sent out by earthquakes. Several seismometers are placed around a volcano to measure how often the quakes are coming, where they're coming from and how big they are. Also used for detecting lahars.

2 Electronic distance meter

Function: Measuring horizontal ground movements.

How it works: It shoots out an infrared laser beam that hits a reflector high up on the volcano and bounces back. From the time this takes, vulcanologists can work out if the volcano has budged. It can detect a change of one measly millimetre over 1 kilometre.

3 Electronic tiltmeter

Function: Measuring vertical ground movements

How it works: It looks like a long tube with a bubble in the middle that's filled with fluid. If the ground, and the fluid, shifts, it sets off an electronic signal. It's placed in a deep hole drilled as high up on the summit as possible.

4 Global Positioning System (GPS)

Function: Measuring ground movements

How it works: Satellites monitor ground movements and beam the information to receivers on the volcano so that vulcanologists can tell their precise position. The same type of system's used in cars for finding the way from A to B. Satellites are also horribly useful for tracking ash and gas clouds, and for making temperature maps.

5 Correlation spectrometer

Function: Measuring volcanic gases

How it works: It's strapped into a car or onto a plane, then driven or flown through a gas plume. It uses ultraviolet light to measure how much sulphur dioxide's belching out. A new, mini version called Flyspec is being tried out in Hawaii.

6 Thermocouple

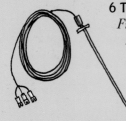

Function: Measuring lava temperatures

How it works: It's like a lava thermometer. You stick a long probe into the lava, then read its temperature on a hand-held device. Simple as that.

VILE VOLCANO 5: PINATUBO

L ast stop on your vile volcanic tour is perilous Mount Pinatubo in the Philippines. It's one of a long line of active volcanoes streaking across the island of Luzon. In 1991, Pinatubo had been dormant for at least 400 years, and no one thought it would erupt again. And then, the volcano exploded violently and gave everyone the shock of their lives. Luckily, vulcanologists monitoring the mountain were on top of things and spotted the warning signs. Just in time, they ordered the area to be evacuated, saving tens of thousands of lives.

PIN YOUR HOPES ON PINATUBO!

VILE VOLCANO FACT FILE

Name: **Pinatubo**
Location: **Philippines**
Type: **Stratovolcano**
Last major eruption: **1991 (VEI 6)**
Last eruption: **1993**
Height (before 1991): **1,745 metres**
Height (after 1991): **1,485 metres**
Status: **Active**

Pinatubo facts

- The 1991 eruption was ten times more violent than Mount St Helens, making it the second largest in the 20th century next to Novarupta, Alaska, in 1912.
- It spewed out 20 million tonnes of sulphur dioxide. The gas took three weeks to travel around the world, making the global temperature around 0.5°C colder.
- Its slopes were once covered in thick rainforest and were home to tens of thousands of local people called the Aeta.
- The eruption blew the top off the mountain, leaving a crater 2 kilometres across.

BOOM!

Pinatubo: Volcano visitor's guide

- **Getting there:**

It's a bumpy drive across the muddy slopes, then a three-hour hike up a trail to the summit. But check with the authorities before you go. Pinatubo's still horribly dangerous, and visitors have only just been allowed back to the mountain again.

- **Where to stay:**

The closest village is Santa Juliana where the drive begins. Or, if you're feeling brave, you can pitch a tent on the still-ashy slopes.

- **What to take:**

You'll need a local Aeta guide who'll know the volcano like the back of his hand. Don't forget your swimsuit. The crater's filled with a sparkling turquoise blue lake and you can swim in it, as long as you stay close to the bank.

- **When to go:**

It's best to go in the dry season (January and February) when it's also refreshingly cool. Avoid the rainy season. The rain can set old lahars flowing again, turning rivers into raging torrents and even triggering explosions.

- **Other places to visit:**

Taal: It's another crystal-clear crater lake blasted out by an ancient eruption. Get a boat from the shore to Volcano Island in the middle of the lake. There's another crater lake on the island with another island in the middle. So it's really three volcanoes in one.

Mayon: It's a picture-postcard volcano with a perfect pointy cone. But don't be fooled. It's the most active volcano in the Philippines and has erupted almost 50 times in the last 400 years. So you don't want to get too close.

Evacuation timeline

5 April 1991

The Philippine Institute of Vulcanology sets up seismometers around the volcano. In the first 24 hours, they record a shocking 200 small earthquakes.

7 April 1991

People living within 10 kilometres of the summit are ordered to evacuate.

23 April 1991

A team of vulcanologists arrive from the USA with more monitoring equipment.

13 May 1991

Up to 130 earthquakes are recorded every day.

Vulcanologists issue a warning that the volcano is now at alert level 2 (this means it's active and an eruption's expected). They also show a

video explaining the danger and telling people what to do. Daily updates appear in newspapers and on radio and TV.

23 May 1991

A hazard map is drawn up. It shows the places in danger if the volcano blows.

28 May 1991

Instruments record a tenfold increase in the amount of sulphur dioxide coming from the volcano. Things are really hotting up.

5 June 1991

Earthquakes continue. A bulge appears on the side of the mountain as magma moves menacingly upwards. The alert level's raised to 3 (meaning an eruption's possible in the next two weeks).

7 June 1991

The volcano spews an ash cloud 8 kilometres into the air. 1,500 earthquakes are recorded. The alert level's raised to 4 (meaning an eruption's possible in the next 24 hours).

9 June 1991

The first pyroclastic flows roll down the slopes. The alert level's raised to 5 (meaning an

eruption's in progress). The evacuation zone's extended to 20 kilometres.

13 June 1991

Ash eruptions continue. Pyroclastic flows race down the valleys. The evacuation zone's extended to 30 kilometres. 58,000 people have left their homes.

15 June 1991

The eruption's at its most violent. The ash plume reaches 40 kilometres into the air and spreads out, plunging the region into pitch blackness. The evacuation zone's extended to 40 kilometres. The eruption ends at around 10.30 pm

16 June 1991

Another 200,000 people leave their homes, making this the biggest evacuation in volcano history.

EARTH—SHATTERING FACT

At the same time as the eruption, deadly Typhoon Yunya slammed into the island, making matters much, much worse. The typhoon brought torrential rain, which mixed with the awesome amounts of ash and sent massive lahars crashing down the volcano's slopes. The murderous mud buried whole towns and villages, devastated farmland and clogged up vital river valleys. Worse still, the lahars later returned (see page 29). The shattered region has still not recovered.

Could you be a vulcanologist?

TEN WAYS TO AVOID BEING BLOWN TO SMITHEREENS

Before an eruption...

DO listen out for warnings on the radio or TV. There are different levels of alert, depending on what the volcano's doing. If you're in the vilely volcanic USA, here's the system you'll be hearing:

Volcanic Alert Levels

Normal: No activity. The volcano's not erupting at present.

Advisory: Some activity. The volcano's being closely monitored.

Watch: More action with an eruption possible. A small eruption might already be underway.

Warning: A violent eruption's underway with serious hazards likely.

DO pack an emergency survival kit. You'll need water and tinned food (don't forget a tin opener), a first-aid kit, torch (with spare batteries), a dust mask and pair of goggles, spare clothes and a pair of sturdy boots or shoes.

During an eruption...
If you're caught indoors...

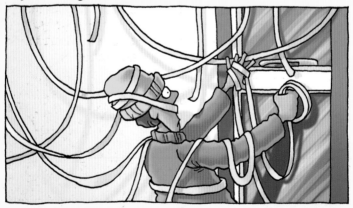

DO close all the windows and doors to stop ash and hot cinders coming in. Tape draughty windows shut and put damp, rolled-up towels under the doors.

If you're caught outdoors...

DO get to high ground, away from the volcano. Then you're out of reach of lahars and pyroclastic flows heading downhill.

DON'T try to outrun a lahar. Whatever you do. It can flow much faster than you can run and you'll be buried under tonnes of mud.

If you're caught in an ashfall...

DO wear a dust mask or hold a damp hanky over your mouth and nose. And wear goggles or glasses to protect your eyes.

DO keep your skin covered to stop the ash burning or irritating it. Long-sleeved tops and long trousers are a must.

After an eruption...

DO clear the ash from your roof. Ash is very heavy and can easily cause your roof, and your house, to cave in.

DON'T drive anywhere if ash is falling. You'll stir the ash up and it'll clog up your engine.

DON'T go outside until you're told it's definitely safe.

HORRIBLE HEALTH WARNING

In November 1985, some 23,000 people lost their lives when Nevado del Ruiz erupted in Colombia. Lethal lahars poured downhill at speeds of up to 40 km/h, sweeping the town of Armero away. It was the worst volcanic disaster of the 20th century but it shouldn't have been. Even though vulcanologists warned local officials of the risk, no evacuation plans were made. In fact, radio stations told people not to panic and advised them to stay at home. By the time any serious warnings were broadcast, most people were fast asleep in bed and it was too late to get out of the way.

EPILOGUE

Congratulations! You've visited some of the most violent volcanoes on Earth on your vile volcanic tour. You've climbed some murderous mountains and survived being blown away. For now, at least. You've been there, done that and you've even got the 'I Lava Volcano' T-shirt (remember Mount St Helens?). So where on Earth do you go from here? If earthly eruptions leave you cold, why not check out some of the vile volcanoes that are huffing and puffing away in outer space? Wouldn't know a cryovolcano* from a Christmas tree? Don't panic. Here's an explosive guide to some horribly cosmic hot spots...

* A cryovolcano is an ice volcano and not a green, pointy tree you put tinsel on.

Five cosmic hot spots

1 Venus

You'll be spoiled for choice if you're visiting Venus. It boasts THOUSANDS of vile volcanoes. Maat Mons is the biggest, at a whopping 8 kilometres tall. Scientists reckoned Venus's volcanoes were long dead. Then pictures from a passing spacecraft showed what looked like ash flows coming from Maat Mons's summit. So, it could be stirring…

2 Mars

Mars is famous for Olympus Mons, the biggest volcano IN THE KNOWN UNIVERSE. It's three times taller than massive Mauna Loa on Earth and an astonishing 650 kilometres wide. And it doesn't stop there. This vast shield volcano is topped by a colossal crater the size of a city. Luckily, this monster mountain has been extinct for around 200 million years.

3 Io

Want to visit the most volcanic place in space? Head for explosive Io (one of Jupiter's moons) – it's jam-packed with volcanoes. And they're all horribly ACTIVE, spewing out lava flows 500 kilometres long and plumes of gas 500 kilometres high. Actually, all of this lava and gas makes the surface of Io look more like a mouldy orange than a lump of space rock.

4 Europa

Europa's another one of Jupiter's moons and if it's cryovolcanoes you're after, you've come to the right place. Instead of red-hot magma, these vile volcanoes spurt out liquids that freeze when they hit Europa's fr-r-r-eezing cold, icy surface. Check out other cryovolcanoes on Triton (a moon of Neptune) and Enceladus (a moon of Saturn).

5 Moon

If you're looking for somewhere a bit closer to home, try the Mare Imbrium on the the Earth's moon. Its name means 'sea of rains' but it's no place for a refreshing dip. It's covered in thick volcanic rock with lava flows up to 1,200 kilometres long, not to mention cosmic clusters of lava domes and cinder cones (remember those?).

EARTH-SHATTERING FACT

You know the saying 'there's plenty more fish in the sea'? The same goes for volcanoes. So far, vulcanologists have counted over 200,000 volcanic vents underwater and there could be millions more. Well, it beats counting sheep, I guess. Most of them simmer away under the surface so you'd never even know they were there. But some poke up to form flaming islands, like Hawaii and Iceland.

Vile volcano watch

Back down to Earth with a bump and some vile volcanoes are getting vulcanologists particularly hot and bothered. They're called Decade Volcanoes and there are 16 of the perishing peaks. They need watching carefully because **a)** they're all horribly active and **b)** they're all horribly close to places where humans like to live.

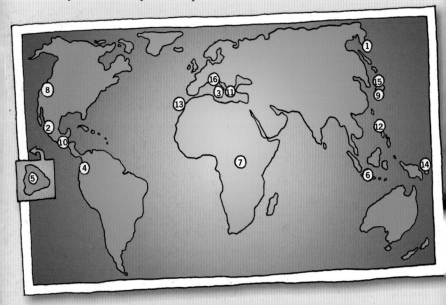

1. Avachinsky–Koryaksky, Russia
2. Colima, Mexico
3. Etna, Italy
4. Galeras, Colombia
5. Mauna Loa, Hawaii
6. Merapi, Indonesia
7. Nyiragongo, Congo
8. Rainier, USA
9. Sakurajima, Japan
10. Santa Maria, Guatemala
11. Santorini, Greece
12. Taal, Philippines
13. Teide, Canary Islands
14. Ulawun, Papua New Guinea
15. Unzen, Japan
16. Vesuvius, Italy

Vile volcanic websites

www.volcanoes.com
Facts about the latest volcanic hot topics, volcano stories and photo galleries.

http://volcano.oregonstate.edu
The Volcano World website, packed with masses of volcanic information and the latest volcanic activity.

http://vulcan.wr.usgs.gov/volcanoes
Links to information on hundreds of vile volcanoes, big and small, from around the world.

www.volcano.si.edu
Check out the Global Volcanism Website to hear the latest volcanic activity reports.

http://hvo.wr.usgs.gov/cam
The website of the Hawaiian Volcano Observatory with live pictures of Kilauea crater.

www.ov.ingv.ot
The website of the Vesuvius Observatory which gives the latest levels of alert.

www.visibleearth.nasa.gov
A sizzling collection of images of volcanoes taken by NASA spacecraft.

www.decadevolcano.com
A photo gallery of spectacular volcanic eruptions, showing many of the volcanoes in this book.

INDEX

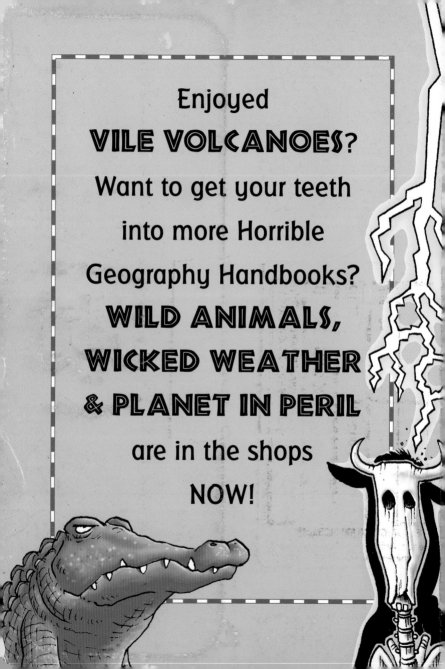